£4.50

BARBIE™ ANNUAL, 1992, is published by **MARVEL COMICS LTD.**, Arundel House, 13/15 Arundel Street, London WC2R 3DX. Printed in Italy. **Editor:** Louise Cassell.

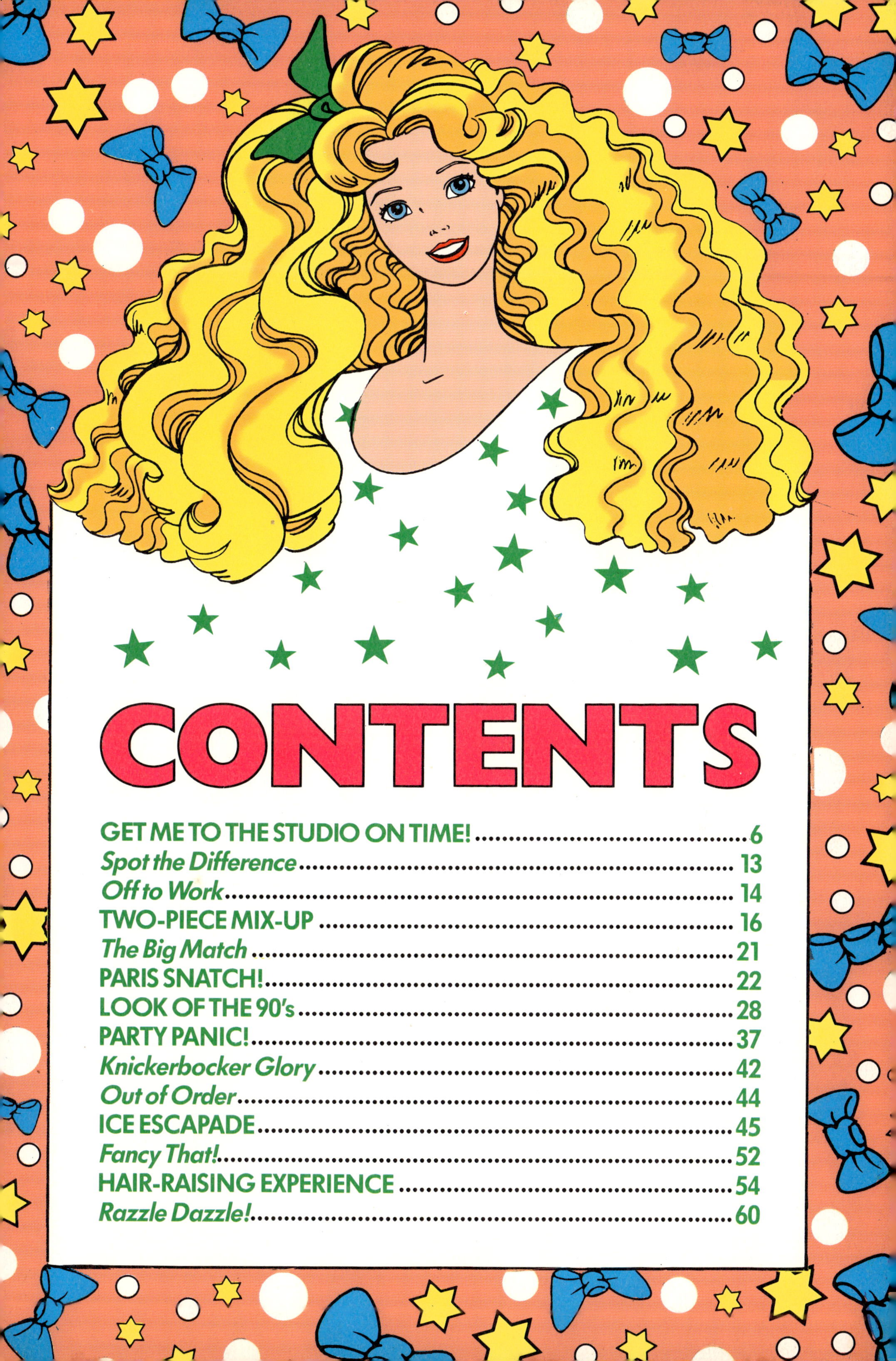

CONTENTS

BARBARA SLATE Writer
AMANDA CONNER Penciler
ANDY MUSHYNSKY, ROY RICHARDSON Inkers
JANICE CHIANG, CHRIS ELIOPOULIS Letterers
EVELYN STEIN, MIKE WORLEY Colorists
FABIAN NICIEZA Editor
TOM DeFALCO Editor in Chief

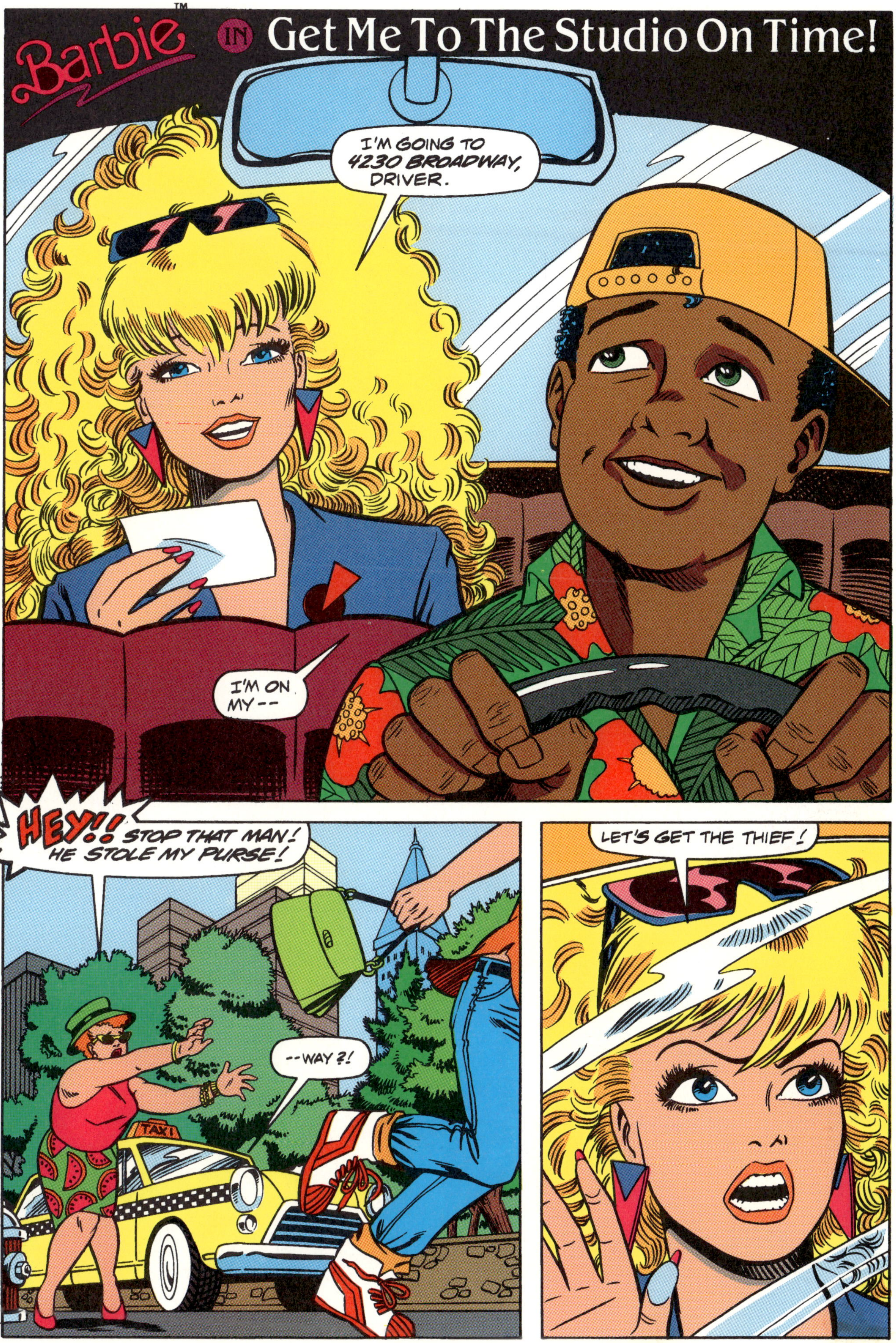

Barbie™ IN Get Me To The Studio On Time!

I'M GOING TO 4230 BROADWAY, DRIVER.

I'M ON MY--

WHICH WAY DID HE GO, GIRLIE?
THAT-A-WAY! AND MY NAME IS BARBIE!
TAXI

THANKS, PARTNER!
PARTNER?!
1.75
CLEAVER, CLYDE
NO SMOKING
PASSENGER RESPONSIBLE FOR
DRIVER NOT REQUIRED TO CHANGE BILLS OVER
DRIVER NOT REQUIRED TO CHANGE DIRTY

GOOD GOIN'!! GET HIM!

STOP THAT MAN, OFFICERS! HE'S A THIEF!

STOP! POLICE!
THANK YOU! YOU'RE MY HEROES!
I'M HAPPY WE COULD HELP.
YEAH... WE'RE A REGULAR TEAM... BARBIE AND CLYDE!

BUT I'M SORRY I WON'T BE ABLE TO DRIVE YOU, BARBIE. MY TAXI'S GOT A FLAT!
DON'T WORRY I STILL CAN GET TO THE STUDIO ON TIME...
GOODBYE AND TAKE CARE OF YOURSELF.
YOU TOO...

...PARTNER!

I'M IN LUCK! HERE COMES A BUS!
BUS STOP

IT'S A GOOD THING I STARTED EXTRA EARLY...

...OTHERWISE I MIGHT BE-- LATE--?
OH NO!!

A PARADE!

NOW WHAT AM I GOING TO DO?

!

SIR, I HAVE TEN MINUTES TO GET TO THE MOST IMPORTANT MODELLING SHOOT OF MY WHOLE LIFE! CAN YOU TAKE ME?
HOP IN!

THE ADDRESS IS 4230 BROAD--

--WAY!

BUT I WANT TO GET THERE IN ONE PIECE, SIR!

I GOT YOU HERE ON TIME AND IN ONE PIECE.
THANK YOU.
WELL, BREAK A LEG!
I ALMOST DID!

JUST THREE MINUTES TO GO!
4230
OADWA

COME ON, ELEVATOR! DON'T FAIL ME NOW!

OH NO! IT'S GOING UP!
1 2 3 4 5 6 7 8 9 10 11 12 13 14 15 16

IF I TAKE THESE STAIRS TWO AT A TIME...

...I STILL SHOULD BE ABLE TO MAKE IT!

IT'S A GOOD THING I'VE BEEN EXERCISING!
8th Floor

STUDIO 4
THERE IT IS! WITH 5 SECONDS TO SPARE!

I'M HERE!!
HI, BARBIE. I'M AFRAID I'VE GOT SOME BAD NEWS. RICARDO CAUGHT THAT 24 HOUR VIRUS...
STUDIO 4

...WE'LL HAVE TO RESCHEDULE THE SHOOT FOR TOMORROW.

I TRIED TO CALL BUT YOU HAD ALREADY LEFT!
I UNDERSTAND, JOYCE... RICARDO GOT A 24 HOUR BUG...
...AND I NEEDED A 24 HOUR HEAD START.

I'VE GOT MY CAR OUTSIDE, BARBIE... DO YOU WANT A RIDE HOME?
NO, THANKS. I THINK I'D BETTER WALK!
CONTINUED ON P.28

SPOT THE DIFFERENCE

Barbie's just been for a trim to the hairdressers, but whilst she's gone to pay for her cut and blow dry, somebody is going to have to clear up the mess! If you look carefully at the second picture, you'll see someone has already started! Try and spot eight differences from the first picture.

ANSWERS: flower, comb, scissor handle, tap head, bottle top, socket, nose on poster, cloth on back of sink

OFF TO WORK!

Help Barbie get to work on time by playing this fast-moving board game with your friends! All you need are some counters and dice. Roll the die and move as many spaces as indicated. Follow the instructions on the squares as you go. The first person to get the exact number to land Barbie at the studio at the finish is the winner!

FINISH
Barbie arrives safely at work!
45
44 RED LIGHT MISS A GO
43
42
41 YOU PICK UP SOME LITTER. MOVE TO Nº 43
40
39 GO THE WRONG WAY. BACK TO Nº 28
38 YOU FIND A SHORT CUT. GO TO Nº 43
37
36 YOU SLIP UP. MISS A GO.
35 GREEN LIGHT EXTRA GO
34
33
32 HELP OLD LADY CROSS THE ROAD. GO TO Nº 37
31 GO THE WRONG WAY. BACK TO Nº 23
30
29
28
27 THANKS TO SPEEDY BUS LANE GO TO Nº 33
26
25
24 YOU SLIP UP. MISS A GO.
23
22
21 CATCH A BUS. GO TO Nº 29
20
19
18 YOU SLIP UP. MISS A GO.

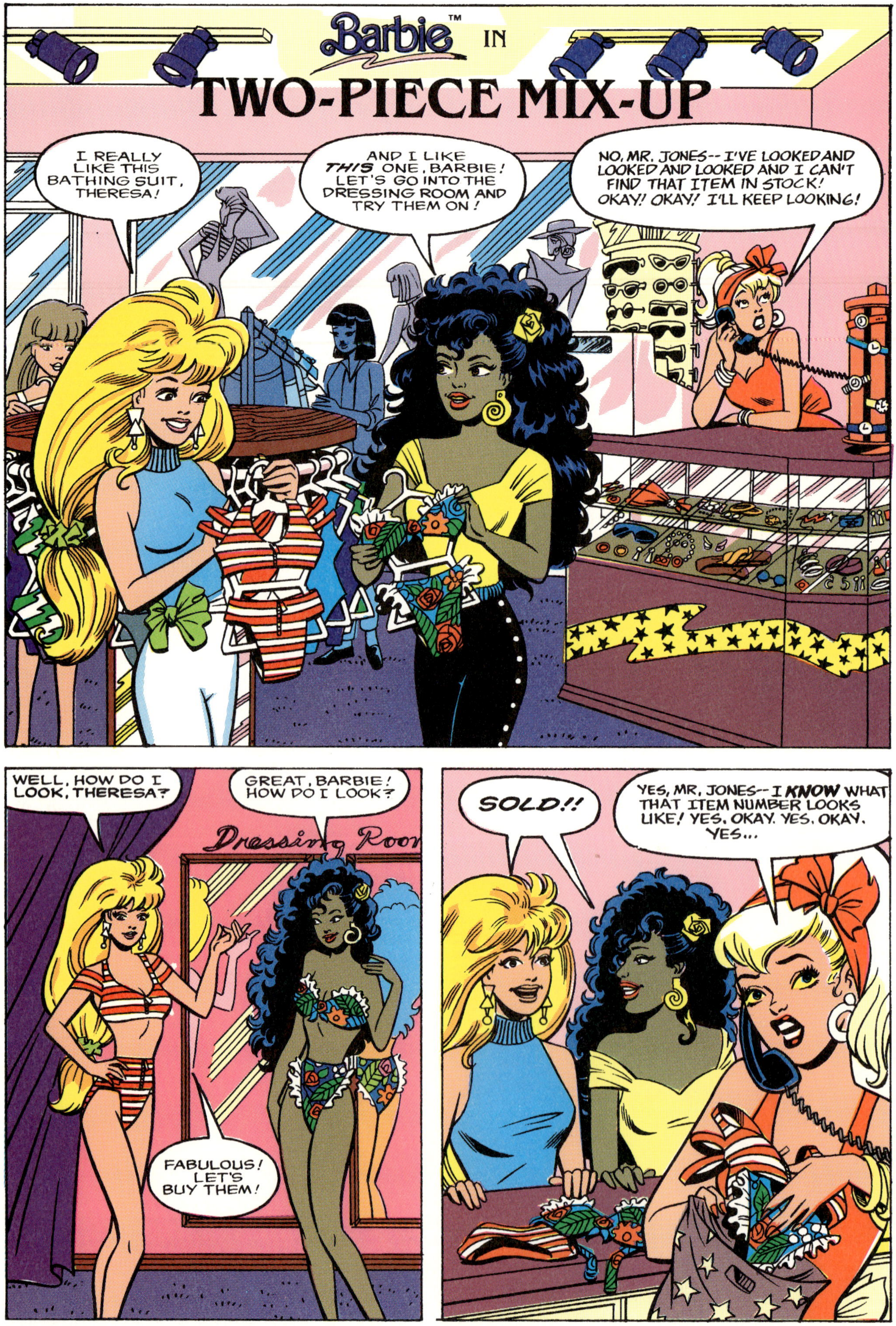

Barbie™ in TWO-PIECE MIX-UP

I REALLY LIKE THIS BATHING SUIT, THERESA!

AND I LIKE *THIS* ONE, BARBIE! LET'S GO INTO THE DRESSING ROOM AND TRY THEM ON!

NO, MR. JONES-- I'VE LOOKED AND LOOKED AND LOOKED AND I CAN'T FIND THAT ITEM IN STOCK! OKAY! OKAY! I'LL KEEP LOOKING!

LATER...
LET'S SEE...WHAT'LL I NEED FOR THE BEACH? TOWEL... SUNTAN LOTION...

MY STRAW HAT, HAIR BRUSH, SUNGLASSES, AND OF COURSE...

MY NEW BATHING--

--SUIT?! OMIGOODNESS! THIS TOP BELONGS TO THERESA!

DING DONG

THAT MUST BE KEN! OH, WELL! I'LL JUST HAVE TO MAKE DO!

AT THE BEACH...
TONIGHT AT THE CATTLE CLUB-B-1 BOMBERS
GOOD SHOT, BARBIE!
DO YOU SEE THAT GIRL'S BATHING SUIT?
YES! IT DOESN'T MATCH!
I THINK IT LOOKS SILLY, DON'T YOU?
I'LL SAY! DOESN'T SHE REALIZE HER SUIT IS MIXED UP?
LIFEGUARD
LATER...
THIS WAS A WONDERFUL DAY AT THE BEACH, KEN!
YES IT WAS, BARBIE! I HAD A GREAT TIME!

HI, THERESA! IT'S BARBIE!
HI, BARBIE! DID YOU AND KEN HAVE A NICE DAY AT THE BEACH?

YES, WE DID, THERESA... BUT HAVE YOU LOOKED INSIDE YOUR BAG AT YOUR BATHING SUIT?

OMIGOODNESS! YOU HAVE THE TOP OF MY TWO-PIECE!

IF THAT POOR SALESWOMAN HADN'T BEEN SO BUSY THIS WOULDN'T HAVE HAPPENED!

I THINK YOU'RE RIGHT, THERESA! I'D LIKE TO COME OVER RIGHT AWAY AND PICK UP MY TOP!

KEN AND I ARE GOING TO THE BEACH AGAIN TOMORROW, AND I WANT MY TWO-PIECE TO MATCH!

THE NEXT DAY AT THE BEACH...
YOU REALLY KNOW HOW TO SET THE FASHION TREND, BARBIE!
THE END

THE BIG MATCH

Barbie and Skipper are both dressed up to go out! Barbie is going to a glamorous party with some of her friends from the world of fashion, whilst Skipper is taking the dog for a walk in the park. Before they go, help them sort out which accessories belong to whom. There are four to go with each outfit.

ANSWER: *Barbie* – Gloves, jewellery, feather boa, bag ***Skipper*** – Leggings, scarf, bobble hat, ear muffs

PARIS SNATCH

"Wow! So this is Paris! It's ace!" Skipper stood at the rails of the tourist boat as it steered its way along the murky waters of the River Seine. She could see the ornate twin towers of the great French cathedral, *Notre Dame*, which stood out against the blue skyline.

"Yes, I was lucky to be invited to the Paris fashion show," agreed Barbie, enjoying the cool breeze on her face. "Paris is one of the most romantic and exciting cities in the world!"

Ken was busy taking photographs of Barbie for a new book he was hoping to publish about the beautiful young fashion model.

"Turn a little to the right, Barbie. . . that's it. . . chin up. . . brilliant!"

"Oh, Ken!" laughed Barbie. "You can get pictures of me any time. You should be soaking up the beauties of Paris instead!" She pointed to the great cathedral as it came into view. "Take *Notre Dame*, for instance. It was built from 1163 to 1250, and has survived the French Revolution, and two World Wars!"

Skipper was more interested in looking at the young frenchmen who walked along the banks of the Seine!

"I can't wait to hit some of the nightclubs," she said, hopefully, as the boat pulled into a jetty, and they joined the queue of eager sightseers who were shuffling slowly down the gangplank.

"Skipper! You're terrible!" chuckled Barbie. "Still, I'll see what we can do. But first, I'd better get to the hotel. The dress rehearsal starts in half an hour."

They hailed a taxi, and were soon back at their four-star, deluxe hotel, the *Residence Maxim's de Paris*.

"*Mademoiselle* Barbie! Ze rehearsal! It ees about to start! You are late, non?" cried Pierre Duval, the show's highly temperamental organiser, who was standing in the crowded hotel foyer. He clapped his hands, sharply. "Hurry, please! Ze dress – it ees waiting for you in ze *cabines d'essayage*!"

"He means the dressing room!" laughed Barbie, as Skipper gave her a quizzical stare. "You should swot up in your french classes more, Skipper!"

As Barbie made her way to the dressing rooms, she was watched by a tall man, who was dressed in a dark trenchcoat and hat. He was skulking behind a large display of flowers that had been ordered for the show.

"Zis Briteesh model! She is ze one! With her unwitting 'elp, I, Jacques Nick-Nack, shall smuggle ze jewels I stole out of France! No one weel suspect a famous fashion model of being a jewel thief! Ha, ha, ha!"

"You look great, Barbie!" said Ken, who had already used up two rolls of film in taking pictures of Barbie in the magnificent dress she was wearing for the fashion show. It was a red velvet, formal evening dress, decorated with a sparkling display of imitation diamonds!

"And Pierre says I can keep the dress when I've finished modelling it!" said Barbie, excitedly. "There's not another one like it in Britain!"

"You always were a trend-setter, Barbie!" said Skipper. "But you'd better swing it! I can hear Pierre calling for you!"

Barbie spent the next hour learning what Pierre wished her to do at the fashion show, that evening.

When the dress rehearsal had finished, she returned the dress to her hotel room, and then went shopping to the boutiques with Skipper.

"Now ees ze time!" decided Jacques Nick-Nack, as he watched Barbie descend in the elevator. Using a skeleton key, he unlocked the door of Barbie's room. Quickly, he found the dress, removed all the imitation diamonds, and replaced them with *real* diamonds!

"Now I must get out of here!" muttered Nick-Nack. "Ze *gendarmes*, zey are 'ot on my 'eels!"

Nick-Nack slipped out of Barbie's room just as Barbie returned, carrying

a dozen large shopping bags, full of the latest French fashions.

"Hey! What do you think you're doing?" she shouted.

At the same time, a young police officer, a *gendarme*, appeared in the corridor. There had been reports of a suspicious character hanging around the hotel, and he had come to investigate. He immediately recognised Jacques Nick-Nack from the police files.

"Nick-Nack! Ze international jewel thief!" he gasped. "I shall get a promotion for capturing him!"

"*Sacré Bleu*! I am in ze trouble!" gasped Nick-Nack, as the *gendarme* ran towards him. Before Barbie could understand what was happening, Nick-Nack grabbed her roughly by the shoulders, and threw her into the police officer's path.

"**Whooof**!" gasped Barbie, as they both fell to the floor in a tangle of arms and legs and shopping bags.

"*Au revoir, Mademoiselle*! It was nice doing ze business with you!" laughed Nick-Nack. He pushed aside Skipper, and ran down the stairs.

By the time the police officer had picked himself up, Nick-Nack had vanished!

"Zis is your fault!" he accused Barbie. "You helped him to escape!"

"I did not!" said Barbie, indignantly. "I don't even know him!"

Barbie could see the *gendarme* did not believe her. He escorted her back to her room.

"What ees thees about doing 'business' with you?" he said, suspiciously. Before Barbie could answer, he glanced at the dress on Barbie's bed. Examining the dress more closely, he let out a gasp of surprise.

"Zese are diamonds!"

Barbie laughed. "Silly! They are only imitation!"

The police officer shook his head. "*Non*! I know real diamonds when I see zem! You must be Nick-Nack's accomplice! I suppose you were going to smuggle them back to Britain in zis dress!"

"No!" gasped Barbie, who also recognised that the diamonds were real ones. "The crook must have switched them while I was out shopping!"

"A likely tale!" scoffed the *gendarme*. "*Mademoiselle* Barbie – *you are under arrest*!"

"Officer, please listen to me! I'm a fashion model, not a thief! Give me a chance to clear my name! I have a plan to catch *Monsieur* Nick-Nack and prove my innocence! Let me come to the police station with you and explain everything to your superior!"

The young officer agreed, and shortly, Barbie and Skipper were whisked away to a secret meeting with the Chief of Police . . .

Later that afternoon, a suspicious looking figure watched from across the road as Barbie and Skipper were marched down the steps of the police station under police escort.

But suddenly, the scene changed as Skipper seemed to trip up. Whilst the two officers bent over to help her, Barbie slipped from their grasp and Skipper dived through their legs to make a daring escape. They hailed a passing taxi and sped away from the scene!

"Oh la, la!" chuckled Jacques Nick-Nack to himself from across the road, "I never thought zese Breetish girls would be so daring! But I will give chase, and when I catch zem, zey will tell me where ze dress has been taken, or else. . ."

He jumped in front of a passing taxi which screeched to a halt. "Follow zat taxi!" he cried.

Jacques Nick-Nack's taxi wound through the heavy Parisian traffic, with the driver even steering up on the pavement when there wasn't enough room to get through!

"Sacré Bleu!" gasped Nick-Nack. "I know French drivers are mad, because I am one! But zis is crazy!

"Stop!" he cried with relief, as he noticed Barbie's taxi pull up in front of the Eiffel Tower, and the two girls jump out. He leapt from the taxi, thrust some franc notes into the driver's hand and raced after them as they made for the top.

The panting Nick-Nack reached the top some while later, as he had missed the lift Barbie and Skipper had caught, and had decided to use the stairs.

As he paused for breath, he saw the two girls with their backs towards him, leaning over the railings, and eavesdropped on their conversation.

"It was built in 1889 for a great exhibition," Barbie told Skipper, "and at 300 metres high, weighs 7000 tons! You can see so many marvellous sights from up here too; there's the *Louvre*, the famous art gallery, and to your left is the *Champs Elysées*, the celebrated avenue where the Bastille Day parade is held every year."

"And zis leads to ze *Arc de Triomphe*, built by Emperor Napoleon to celebrate 'is victories over Europe between 1800 and 1812," said a sugar-toned voice from behind them.

Barbie and Skipper spun round in horror to find themselves faced by a menacing looking Jacques Nick-Nack!

"You might have been able to escape from ze police, but not from me," he hissed. "Now, tell me where

ze dress is, or it weel be ze worst for you!" he threatened as he closed in on Barbie and Skipper.

As the two girls looked vainly for a way to escape, a large party of American tourists poured out of the lift, which had just opened nearby. In the confusing crowd, Barbie and Skipper dashed for the lift.

"Back to the hotel Skipper!" Barbie cried, as they barged past the bewildered and frustrated Nick-Nack, who determined to follow them as soon as the next lift reached the top.

"So, zey are going back to ze hotel to get ze dress, I'll bet. Well, so will I. And zis time I will corner zem; Jacques Nick-Nack does not get fooled twice!"

A short time later, a tall, bearded *gendarme* slipped unnoticed into the foyer of the hotel, which was swarming with anxious policemen.

"Hah, hah!" Nick-Nack chuckled to himself. "I knew my disguise would work. All zese *gendarmes* are on ze look-out for *Mademoiselle* Barbie and her young accomplice! But I will find zem first!"

At that moment, Nick-Nack noticed a movement out of the corner of his eye. The swing door into the flamboyant banquet room, where the fashion show was to be held, had gently closed. And sure enough, Nick-Nack noticed the two anxious faces of Barbie and Skipper peering through the round glass windows in the door, before they disappeared out of sight again.

"I will 'ave them now," Nick-Nack muttered to himself, as he strolled as casually as he could over to the door, before slipping into the banquet room, to be faced by a horrified Barbie and Skipper.

"Oh, no!" groaned Barbie. "We're done for!" The two girls ran for cover behind the racks of dresses lined up for the fashion show later that evening.

"No more Meester Nice Guy!" growled Nick-Nack as he gave chase. "Give me zose diamonds!"

"You don't look very fashionable, Jacques," said Barbie. "Here! Try a dress – in fact try a whole rack of them!"

She pushed one of the racks very hard. It slid across the room on wheels, and crashed into Nick-Nack, knocking him off his feet!

"Now the shoe's on the other foot!" laughed Barbie, throwing a box of expensive, imitation crocodile shoes at Nick-Nack before he could recover.

"Let's sock it to him!" giggled Skipper, hitting Nick-Nack with a multi-coloured knee length sock that was still on the leg of a dummy!

"Ouch! Eeek! Ouch! I surrender," wailed Nick-Nack, putting his hands up in defeat.

Just to make sure, Barbie bound his feet and hands with ties. "Hah! This case is all tied up," she laughed as the defeated diamond thief struggled at her feet.

"But you 'ave nothing to laugh about! Ze police are after you too, so we will all go down together!" Nick-Nack cackled triumphantly.

"That's what you think!" laughed Barbie, as to Nick-Nack's surprise, she took a small silver whistle out of her pocket and blew three sharp blasts on it. Seconds later, the *gendarmes* burst into the Banquet Hall, and much to Nick-Nack's surprise, instead of pouncing on Barbie, started clapping and cheering!

The Chief of Police walked towards the group and leant over Nick-Nack.

"*Mademoiselle* Barbie is a guest in our city, and a famous fashion model! How could we possibly think her a thief? When she explained everything to me, we made a plan to lure you into the open, and as you can see, it worked perfectly! Thanks to Barbie and Skipper, Paris will not be seeing your thieving ways again for quite some time!"

As the muttering Nick-Nack was lead away, Barbie and Skipper shook hands with all the cheering *gendarmes* who happily accepted invitations to the fashion show later that night, to celebrate their victory against crime!

"I'm glad that's over!" chuckled Barbie after the diamonds had been removed, and the imitation ones sewn back in place on the dress. "It's time for the show to go on!"

As Barbie stepped out into the spotlight before the audience, she was greeted by a roar of approval.

Skipper, Ken and Pierre Duval watched from backstage. "She ees fabulous!" cried Pierre, happily.

"I know!" chuckled Ken, as he snapped away on his camera. "But Barbie doesn't need real jewels to sparkle! She's a 24-carat gem!"

Story: John Gatehouse **THE END**

Barbie™ IN Look of the 90's
BARBIE, I'D LIKE YOU TO MEET RICARDO. HE WILL BE TAKING YOUR PICTURE FOR THE COVER OF "HERE COMES THE BRIDE" MAGAZINE.
I'M SO HAPPY TO BE WORKING WITH SUCH A FAMOUS PHOTOGRAPHER... AND I'M GLAD YOU'RE FEELING BETTER, RICARDO.
I'M HAPPY TO BE WORKING WITH YOU TOO, BARBIE.
BARBIE HAS BLUE EYES. A NICE PASTEL BLEND SHOULD DO.
OH GREAT! BARBIE HAS BEAUTIFUL LONG HAIR! THAT SHOULD GIVE ME A LOT TO WORK WITH!
HMM... WOULD BARBIE LOOK BETTER IN WHITE OR OFF-WHITE?
TRESS TRENDS
Styling GEL
LESLIE, THE MAKE UP ARTIST
GEORGE, THE HAIRDRESSER
RACHEL, THE STYLIST

THIS COVER HAS TO BE VERY SPECIAL BECAUSE I'M LOOKING FOR THE "BRIDE LOOK OF THE 90'S."
JOYCE, THE EDITOR
OH, THAT'S EASY, JOYCE! THE LOOK OF THE 90'S IS THE ROMANTIC LOOK.
WHAT ?! THE LOOK OF THE 90'S IS THE EGYPTIAN LOOK!
YOU'RE BOTH WRONG! THE BRIDE LOOK OF THE 90'S IS THE 60'S!
ROMANTIC! EGYPTIAN! 60'S! WHAT'S AN EDITOR TO DO?!
I KNOW! WE'LL TRY THEM ALL! LET'S START WITH THE ROMANTIC LOOK!

THAT'S GREAT, BARBIE! NOW SMILE!
CLICK CLICK
AHHH! YES! THE LOOK OF THE 90'S IS THE ROMANTIC LOOK!
BARBIE LOOKS BEAUTIFUL! BUT WAIT TILL YOU SEE THE EGYPTIAN LOOK!
THE 60'S WILL BE EVEN MORE EXCITING!
HMMM... BARBIE LOOKS WONDERFUL IN THIS ROMANTIC STYLE! THIS IS THE ONE!

2 HOURS LATER...
GREAT, BARBIE!
SNAP
CLICK
THAT'S IT! THE EGYPTIAN LOOK! IT'S THE LOOK OF THE 90'S!
YEAH, 90 B.C.
WAIT TILL YOU SEE THE 60'S!
BARBIE LOOKS GREAT IN THE EGYPTIAN STYLE THIS IS THE ONE!
ALL OF YOU HAVE BEEN WORKING VERY HARD. LET'S STOP FOR A LUNCH BREAK.
I STILL SAY THE ROMANTIC LOOK IS THE MOST BEAUTIFUL.
NO, NO... IT'S THE EGYPTIAN LOOK!
NO WAY! IT'S THE 60'S LOOK!

I WISH YOU'D ALL STOP ARGUING!
ALL BRIDES ARE BEAUTIFUL! IT'S THEIR WEDDING DAY!
LOOK!
EVEN A T-SHIRT WEDDING DRESS LOOKS GOOD!
CLICK
CLICK

HA HA HA!
A T-SHIRT FOR A WEDDING GOWN!
NOW THAT'S FUNNY!

BARBIE IS RIGHT! EVERY BRIDE IS BEAUTIFUL! IT'S SILLY TO ARGUE.

OF COURSE YOU'RE RIGHT, RICARDO.
NO NEED TO ARGUE.
WE WERE JUST HELPING THE CREATIVE FLOW.

WELL, IT'S TIME TO GET BACK TO WORK NOW. I'M GLAD WE ALL AGREE.
I STILL SAY IT'S EGYPTIAN!
I STILL SAY IT'S ROMANTIC!
I STILL SAY IT'S 60'S!

BARBIE LOOKS FAB IN THE 60'S! THIS IS THE ONE.
YES, YES!! IT'S THE 60'S!
CLICK
CLICK
THANK YOU, EVERBODY, BUT IT'S TIME TO STOP NOW. YOU ALL DID A WONDERFUL JOB!
TOO WONDERFUL! I DON'T KNOW WHICH IS THE LOOK OF THE 90'S!
GOODBYE, BARBIE!
YOU'RE A GREAT MODEL!
IT'S BEEN FUN WORKING WITH YOU!
GOODBYE AND THANK YOU!
I REALLY ENJOYED WORKING WITH YOU, RICARDO.
YOU'RE A REAL PROFESSIONAL MODEL, BARBIE.

3 WEEKS LATER...
RING!
HELLO?
HELLO, BARBIE. IT'S RICARDO.

PARK
"HERE COMES THE BRIDE" MAGAZINE HAS HIT THE NEWSSTAND.

I CAN'T WAIT TO SEE IT! WHAT LOOK DID JOYCE CHOOSE FOR THE LOOK OF THE 90'S?

WHY DON'T YOU SEE FOR YOURSELF, BARBIE?
NEWSSTAND
ROMANTIC?! EGYPTIAN?! 60'S?!

OMIGOODNESS! THE T-SHIRT LOOK!
HERE COMES THE BRIDE
I SPIE
CARS & HOT RODDER
End.

"What a wonderful idea this is," said Christie, as she helped Barbie to hang up swathes of bunting and colourful balloons in a large hall. "Fancy having a fashion party to launch the new dress design by your favourite fashion designer, Linda. Even the mayor's attending!"

Barbie was struggling to tie a knot in a large balloon she had just blown up. The balloon slipped out of her fingers, and whizzed around the hall, making a rude raspberry noise.

Rassssp!

Everyone laughed and ducked as the balloon flew over their heads.

"Yes, I can't wait to see it!" said Barbie, chuckling as the balloon hit Ken on the back of the head. "Linda calls it a 'Barbie original'. She says it's the best dress she's designed so far."

"Well, if it's that good I'll certainly be ordering some for my shop, 'Christie's Creations'" said Christie, excitedly. "And this party is a great way to show off the design. All the top fashion companies, models, and fashion reporters will be here tonight."

Ken was helping Midge and Theresa, two other models, and Barbie's close friends, to organise the tables around the hall, so that there was enough room for dancing.

The stage at the end of the hall had been set up with stagelights for when Barbie appeared in Linda's new dress.

"Don't forget, the party's also for the launch of my new photo book – 'Barbie: Biography of a Fashion Model' thats being published next week!" Ken reminded them. "Those pictures I took of Barbie in Paris clinched the deal for me!"

"It's going to be quite a party," agreed Barbie, grinning. "I love an excuse to dance and have some fun!"

"Well, it won't be much of a party if we don't rustle up some food," Skipper reminded her. "We've got a lot of baking to do before tonight! Let's hit the kitchen, gang!"

When everyone had gone, Samantha Greensleeves, Barbie's rival in the fashion world, sneaked into the hall. Her eyes burned with envy when she saw the preparations for the party.

"Linda should have made that dress for me! I'd look much better in it than stupid old Barbie! She thinks she's the Queen of the fashion world with all the attention she gets! But I'll get even with her! When I've finished, this will be the worst night of Barbie's life!"

"I'm glad we decided to supply the food, rather than get outside caterers for the job," said Barbie, now dressed in an apron, with her hair tied in a ponytail. She was busy putting the finishing touches to a bowl of trifle. "It's much more fun doing the baking ourselves!"

"That's fine for you to say," groaned Midge, her hands deep in a bowl of sticky dough. "I've been known to burn cornflakes, and blow up rice puddings!"

Skipper was squirting cream from an icing gun onto a tray of fairy cakes. "Don't worry, Midge! With me around, it'll be a piece of *cake*!" she joked – and then accidently pushed the icing gun handle too hard! **Squiiidge**! Cream splurted out of the gun, and smacked Theresa in the face!

"Thanks, Skipper!" she chuckled, wiping off the cream, and licking it off her fingers. "But I usually prefer *face* cream on my face!"

Ken had made a delicious Black Forest gateau for the party. "It looks so scrumptious I could eat it now!" said Christie, slurping hungrily.

"Well, you'll have to wait," said Ken, playfully slapping her hand with a wooden spoon. "If we start nibbling the food now, there won't be any left for the party."

The friends spent all afternoon preparing for the party. By the time they had finished, they had made dozens of trifles, jellies, cream cakes, and sandwiches.

"Phew! That's the lot!" said Barbie, happily. "Now I'd better get back to the dressing room. Linda will be arriving with my dress, shortly."

Unknown to Barbie, Linda had already arrived, and Samantha Greensleeves was waiting outside to greet her.

"Er, Barbie's busy!" she said, quickly, snatching the large cardboard box from Linda. "I'll, um, make sure she gets this!"

"Make sure that you do," said Linda. "I can't wait to see what Barbie looks like tonight."

Samantha gave a low chuckle. "Neither can I!"

When Linda had left, Samantha hid the box in the boot of her car. Then she took out another box, and returned to the dressing room.

"Ha, ha! Barbie will have a surprise when she sees what she'll be wearing tonight," she chuckled. "If I can't wear Linda's dress, no one will!"

She could hear Barbie singing in the shower. Her clothes were draped over a chair in the dressing room.

"Oh, this is perfect!" giggled Samantha, scooping up the clothes. "The party starts in half an hour. If I take Barbie's clothes, she'll have to wear what's in the box!" And with a final giggle, she put down the box, and sneaked out of the dressing room again.

"Oh, great! Where's the towel? It's freezing in here!" groaned Barbie, staggering around the dressing room, her eyes closed, and water running down her face. "I left it with my clothes!"

She peered unclearly around the room with one eye – and then both eyes sprang open in amazement. "My clothes? Where have they gone?" she gasped, when she saw the empty chair. "I left them right here!"

Barbie hunted around the room, without success. "Humph! If this is Skipper's idea of a joke, I don't think it's funny!" she muttered, crossly. Then she saw the box standing beside the dressing table.

"Oh, well! At least Linda's delivered the dress! I'm almost dry anyway. I'll slip into this. The party's about to start!"

Skipper and Christie were waiting at the entrance of the hall to greet everyone. The hall was already bustling with people waiting to see Linda's latest creation. Ken was sitting in one corner, signing advance copies of his book.

"Where's Barbie?" whispered Christie. "She should be here to greet people! There are some of the top names in the fashion world waiting to meet her, the mayor's arrived – and she's late!"

Skipper was about to reply, when they heard a loud scream coming from the dressing room.

"It's Barbie!" cried Theresa. "Something's wrong!"

The three girls hurried from the hall, along the passage to the dressing room.

"Huh! I bet she's seen a spider or something!" giggled Skipper, as they burst into the room. But the sight they saw made her gasp in amazement.

Barbie stood facing them, dressed in a *scarecrow*'s costume and straw hat!

"*This* is Linda's design?" said a wide-eyed Christie, trying hard not to laugh. "It's, er, very rural!"

"Knock it off!" said Barbie, feeling very embarrassed. "There must have been a mix-up! Linda wouldn't create something like this! Pooh! It smells as if it's just come off a real scarecrow!"

"But what are you going to do?" asked Skipper.

"Well, I can't appear in front of the fashion world dressed like this!" groaned Barbie.

"You'll have to!" said Theresa. "Everybody's waiting to see you! There'll be trouble if you don't appear!"

The crowd in the hall were beginning to grumble.

"Where's Barbie?" said Linda, who was eager to hear what people thought of her new design. "People are getting impatient!"

Samantha Greensleeves smirked. "Perhaps she doesn't like your creation, Linda!" she said, coyly. "You should have let me wear it!"

And then, the doors opened, and in walked Barbie, still dressed as a scarecrow. There were gasps of shock from the crowd. Samantha burst out laughing.

"Barbie?!" cried Linda, feeling very foolish. "What are you playing at?" Barbie was too embarrassed to speak. Then, one by one, people began to laugh.

"Ha, ha! Barbie's having a joke with

us!" chuckled an important fashion buyer.

"Only Barbie could make fun of herself!" chuckled another. "What a good sport she is!"

The hall was filled with clapping and cheering. Barbie smiled in relief. "Phew! They all think I dressed like this on purpose!"

Even Linda saw the funny side to it. "You're right, Barbie!" she said, patting her friend on the back. "Fashion shows do get too serious! It's good to have a joke on ourselves! Well done!"

Samantha, who was standing by the food table, was livid! "I don't believe it!" she fumed, stamping her feet in anger. "Barbie is still getting all the attention!"

She was so angry, she picked up the gateau Ken had made, and threw it at Barbie!

Barbie ducked, and the gateau smacked Christie in the face! **Splaaat**!

"You jealous creep!" yelled Christie, grabbing a trifle, and throwing it at Samantha.

Samantha moved to one side, and the trifle landed on Ken's head! **Splooot**!

"Huh! I suppose you think that's funny!" grumbled Ken, as the cold trifle ran down his back. "Well, have some custard!" He picked up the custard bowl, and tossed the contents towards Christie!

Splooosh! The custard ended up

over three fashion buyers, two reporters, and the mayor!

They all grabbed some food off the table, and threw it at Ken! Soon, the hall was filled with a crazy, chaotic food fight!

Spliisssh! Splaaash! Splooossh!

"Oh, no!" cried Barbie, ducking as a large cream cake sailed over her head. "This fashion party is a disaster!" But she was wrong! Everyone was having a great time!

"Ha, ha! It's like being a little kid again!" chuckled the mayor, pouring a bowl of fruit punch over his wife's head. "Heh! I've always wanted to do that!"

Suddenly, Skipper appeared, holding an exquisite long-flowing yellow dress, decorated with sequined stars, and red rosebuds.

"My dress!" cried a jelly-and-sausage-covered Linda. "Where did you find it?"

"In the back of Samantha's car!" fumed Skipper. Everyone glared at Samantha.

"I'm out of here!" said Samantha, running across the hall. She slipped on a blob of trifle, slid across the floor like a one-legged ice skater, and crashed into the food table, bringing the entire contents crashing down on her.

Barbie pulled her out. Samantha was covered from head-to-foot in trifles, jellies, sandwiches, cakes and salad.

"Heh! Serves you right!" chuckled Midge, as Samantha skulked away with everyone laughing at her.

"This has been the funniest party I've ever been to!" a fashion reporter told Barbie, while a lump of cream ran down his nose. "Now let's see what you look like in Linda's dress!"

Barbie went to the dressing room to put on the dress. When she returned, and walked onto the stage, the hall erupted with loud cheers.

"Your dress is a great success!" Barbie told Linda.

"So are you, Barbie!" chuckled Linda. "So are you!"

Story: John Gatehouse **THE END**

KNICKER BOCKER GLORY

MAKING ICE CREAM. . .

WHAT YOU NEED. . .

* ½ tin of condensed, sweetened milk.
* ½ pint of double cream.
* 2 egg whites.
* Flavourings such as vanilla, coffee, mint or strawberry essence or cocoa powder.
* Decorations such as chopped nuts, chocolate chips, chopped strawberries.

WHAT YOU DO. . .

1. Beat the cream in a bowl until it is quite stiff.
2. In another bowl, whisk the egg whites until they are fluffy and stiff.
3. Add the condensed milk to the cream and carefully mix them together.
4. Add your favourite flavour to the mixture – either a couple of drops of essence, or two dessert spoons of cocoa powder.
5. Add chopped nuts to coffee flavoured ice cream, chocolate chips to mint or chocolate flavoured, strawberries to strawberry flavoured, and anything to vanilla flavoured!
6. Gently fold in the egg whites and put the bowl in a freezer over night.
7. When your ice cream is ready, decorate with anything that's left over, hundreds and thousands or strawberry and chocolate sauces!

MAKING A KNICKERBOCKER GLORY. . .

WHAT YOU NEED. . .

★ Three different coloured ice creams – make them yourself!
★ Different chopped fruits; strawberries, bananas, mandarins.
★ Small pot of whipped cream.
★ A few glace cherries.
★ A chocolate flake, chocolate chips and strawberry or chocolate sauce.

WHAT YOU DO. . .

1. See if your mum has got a proper Knickerbocker Glory glass as shown in the picture. If not, then use an ordinary tall glass, but make sure it's quite strong and, if possible, has a wide top.
2. Either make your own ice cream using the recipe on the other page, or get together three different flavours of ordinary ice cream, say vanilla, chocolate and strawberry.
3. Put one spoonful of chocolate in the bottom and sprinkle with chocolate chips.
4. Next, add a spoonful of vanilla and sprinkle with chopped bananas.
5. Follow this with a spoonful of strawberry and some chopped strawberries.
6. Add another spoonful of vanilla and some chopped mandarins.
7. Finish to the top with chocolate and one final spoon of vanilla, which should pile nicely over the top of the glass.
8. Whip your cream in a bowl, using a whisk. When it is fluffy, drop a big spoonful onto the top!
9. Smother the cream with your favourite sauce and some chocolate chips.
10. Finish with a cherry on the top and stick a flake into the ice cream.

Now, all you need is a long teaspoon and a big appetite, as this is one treat you might have to share with a friend!

OUT OF ORDER

Barbie has some photos of her in six different outfits to send to a magazine. They are for different occasions during the day, but are now in the wrong order. Help Barbie sort them into the right order with the help of the list of outfits below. If you think that No.1, the nightdress matches with picture A, your answer will be 1.A, and so on.

1. *Nightdress* **2.** *Jogging suit to go shopping* **3.** *Business suit for lunchtime meeting* **4.** *Suit for afternoon theatre* **5.** *Cocktail dress for drinks party* **6.** *Evening wear.*

ANSWER: 1E, 2C, 3F, 4A, 5D, 6B

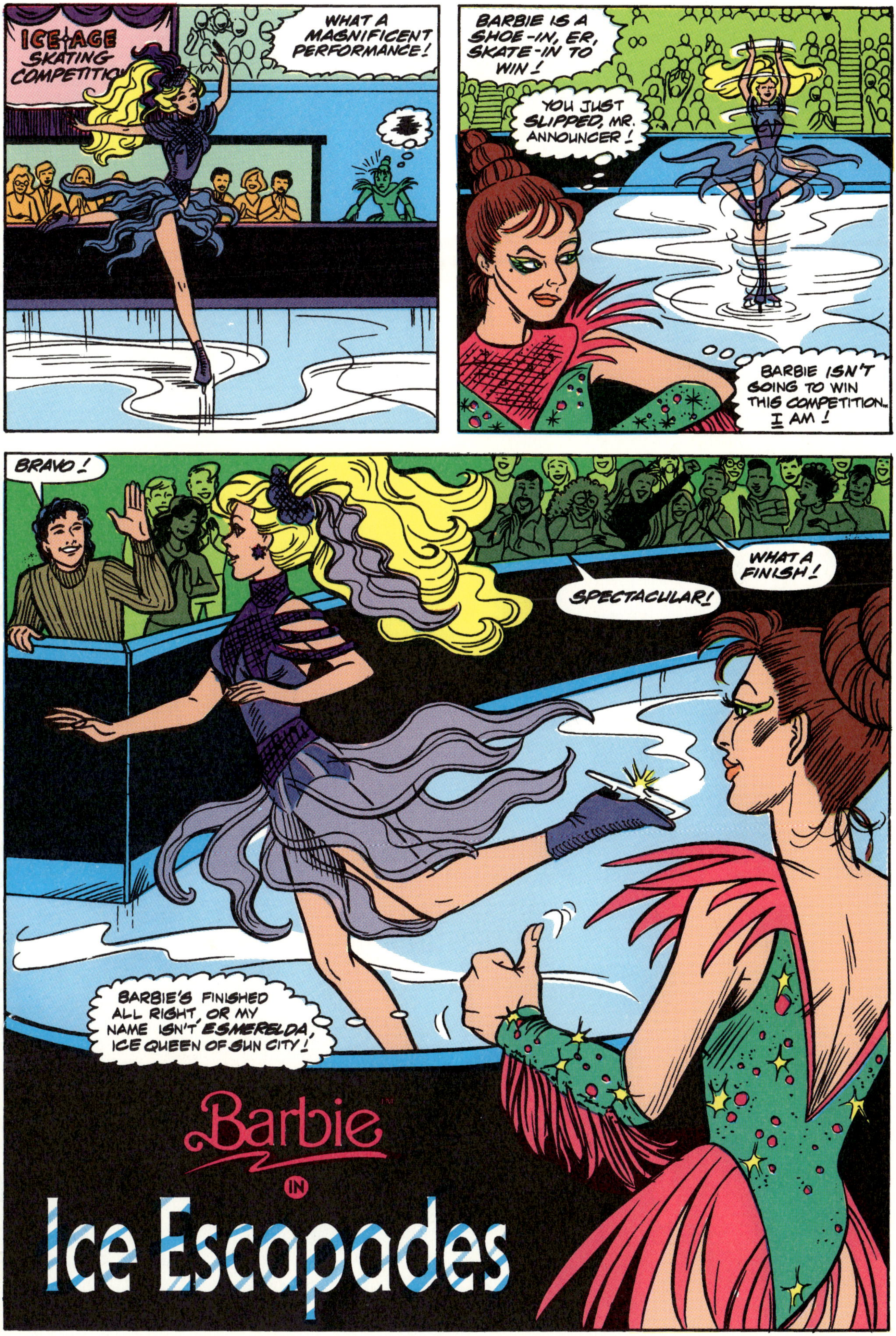

BRAVO!

SPECTACULAR!

WHAT A FINISH!

BARBIE'S FINISHED ALL RIGHT, OR MY NAME ISN'T ESMERELDA, ICE QUEEN OF SUN CITY!

Barbie™ IN Ice Escapades

I THINK YOU MAY WIN WITH THAT PERFORMANCE, BARBIE.
I HOPE SO, KEN.
BUT WHAT I HOPE MOST OF ALL IS THAT...

...SOMEDAY I SKATE AS BEAUTIFULLY AS SONJA STEELE DID IN HER OLD MOVIES.
Sonja Steele
Skate Away
YOU ALREADY DO, DEAR!

WOW! YOU'RE SONJA STEELE!
AND THOSE ARE MY OLD SKATES!

I'VE BEEN FOLLOWING THESE SKATING CHAMPIONSHIPS FOR YEARS...
...AND YOU ARE WONDERFUL, DEAR!

I'D RATHER HAVE A COMPLIMENT FROM YOU THAN A TROPHY ANY DAY!
YOU'LL HAVE BOTH!

BUT YOU WON'T WIN THAT TROPHY UNLESS YOU GET READY FOR YOUR NEXT ROUND.
YOU'RE RIGHT.

PRIVATE
DRESSING ROOM
I HAVE TO CHANGE INTO A NEW COSTUME FOR THE FINAL ROUND.
GOOD LUCK, BARBIE!
HA!
BY THE TIME I'M THROUGH WITH HER, BARBIE'S GOING TO NEED MORE THAN LUCK!

JUST WAIT TILL BARBIE SEES MY COSTUME.

SHE'LL NEVER RECOGNIZE ME!

MEANWHILE...
I'M ON THE CUTTING EDGE WITH THESE MODERN SKATES!
KNOCK KNOCK

WOW! KEN MUST HAVE SENT THESE!
KEN? ER, YES, KEN!

NOW WHERE SHALL I PUT THESE?
I KNOW WHERE I'M GOING TO PUT THESE!

...IN MY DRESSING ROOM!

THAT WAS QUICK! I DIDN'T HAVE A CHANCE TO THANK HIM FOR...
SLAM

...MY SKATES!
hair spray

SOMEONE STOLE MY SKATES!

ICE AGE
IT MUST HAVE BEEN THE DELIVERY BOY!
BUT WHY?

HAVE YOU SEEN A DELIVERY BOY?
WHAT DELIVERY BOY?
SKATE O'RAMA

THE ONE WHO BROUGHT THE FLOWERS YOU SENT ME!
I DIDN'T SEND ANY FLOWERS.

THAT MEANS SOMEONE *PRETENDED* TO BE A DELIVERY BOY SO THEY COULD STEAL MY SKATES!

BARBIE WILL GIVE HER FINAL PERFORMANCE IN FIVE MINUTES.
FIVE MINUTES?!
WHAT ARE YOU GOING TO DO?

YOU CAN'T SKATE IN YOUR SNEAKERS!
MAYBE YOU CAN!

YOU CAN USE MY OLD SKATES.
THEY'LL STRAP ON TO YOUR SNEAKERS!
Sonja Steele
FIRST SKATES 19

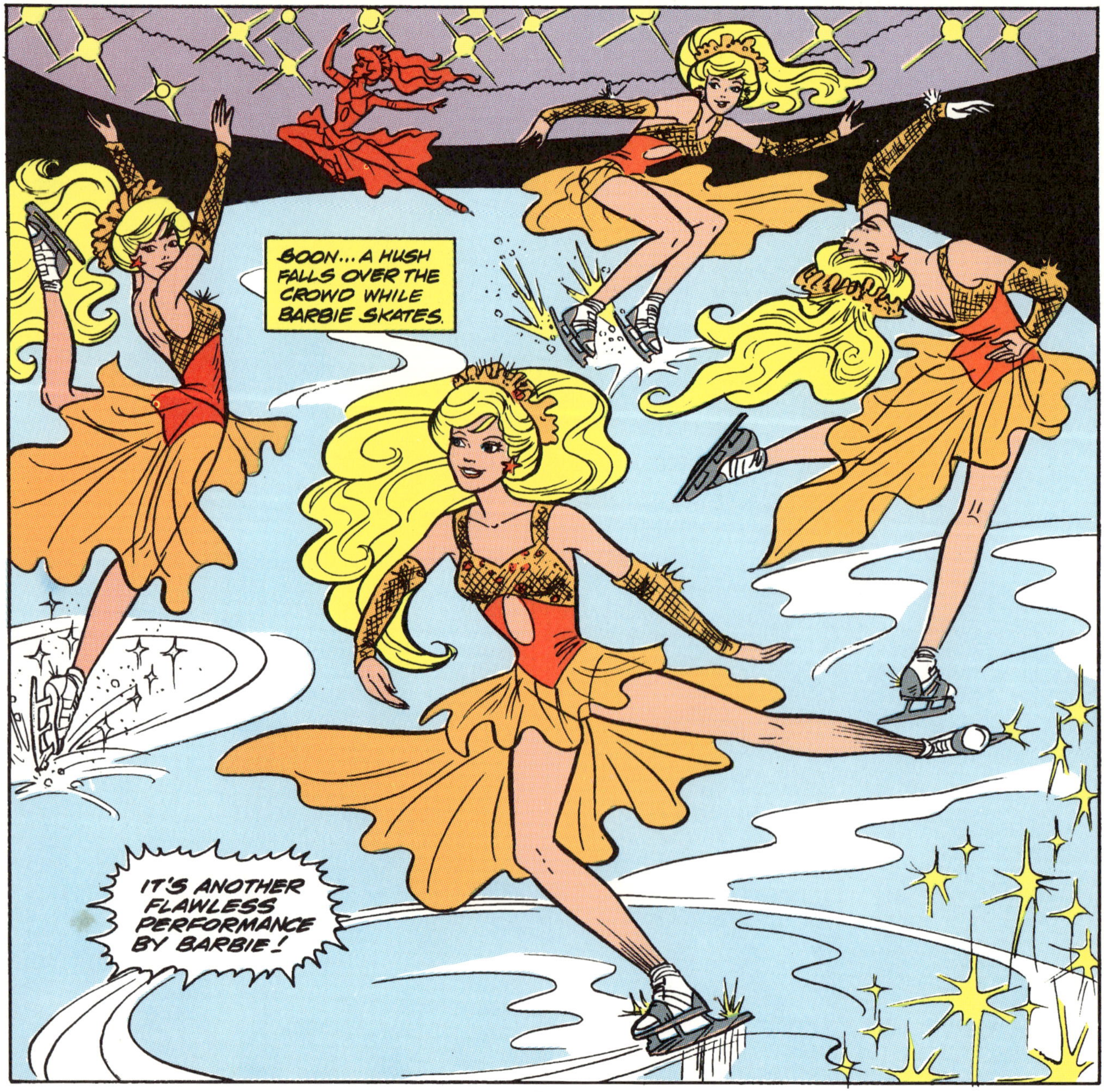

SOON... A HUSH FALLS OVER THE CROWD WHILE BARBIE SKATES.

IT'S ANOTHER FLAWLESS PERFORMANCE BY BARBIE!

LOOKS LIKE THE TROPHY IS YOURS, BARBIE!
THANKS TO SONJA'S WINNING SKATES!

I WONDER WHO TOOK YOUR SKATES.
EVENTS
TO DRESSING ROOM
I THINK I KNOW, KEN.

ESMERELDA, I KNOW YOU STOLE MY SKATES!
?
OH, YEAH?
WHAT PROOF DO YOU HAVE, BARBIE?

IT'S WRITTEN ALL OVER YOUR FACE!
OH, NO, I FORGOT TO REMOVE THE MOUSTACHE!

THERE'S A STIFF PENALTY FOR STEALING SKATES, ESMERELDA!
AND FOR BEING A BAD SPORT!

LATER.
ONLY 999 SKATES LEFT TO SHINE. UGH!
I'VE ALWAYS THOUGHT ESMERELDA'S PERFORMANCE NEEDED MORE POLISH!
THE END.

FANCY

Ken and Barbie have decided to go to a fancy dress party and they've both got a couple of sensational two-in-one, fantasy fashion assortments to choose from! Barbie will go as either a glamorous genie, or if she fancies a change, wear the short, shimmering ballgown skirt and tight, green, spiral underskirt, where she can slip the skirt down to her ankles and become a magical mermaid! Ken must choose between his dazzling dinner suit or making a swift change to a swash-buckling pirate or a genie with a jewelled turban! Once you've matched the clothes correctly, you can trace around the clothes and figures and transfer them onto some thin card. Then colour in the drawings before cutting out the clothes and dressing Ken and Barbie for their big night out!

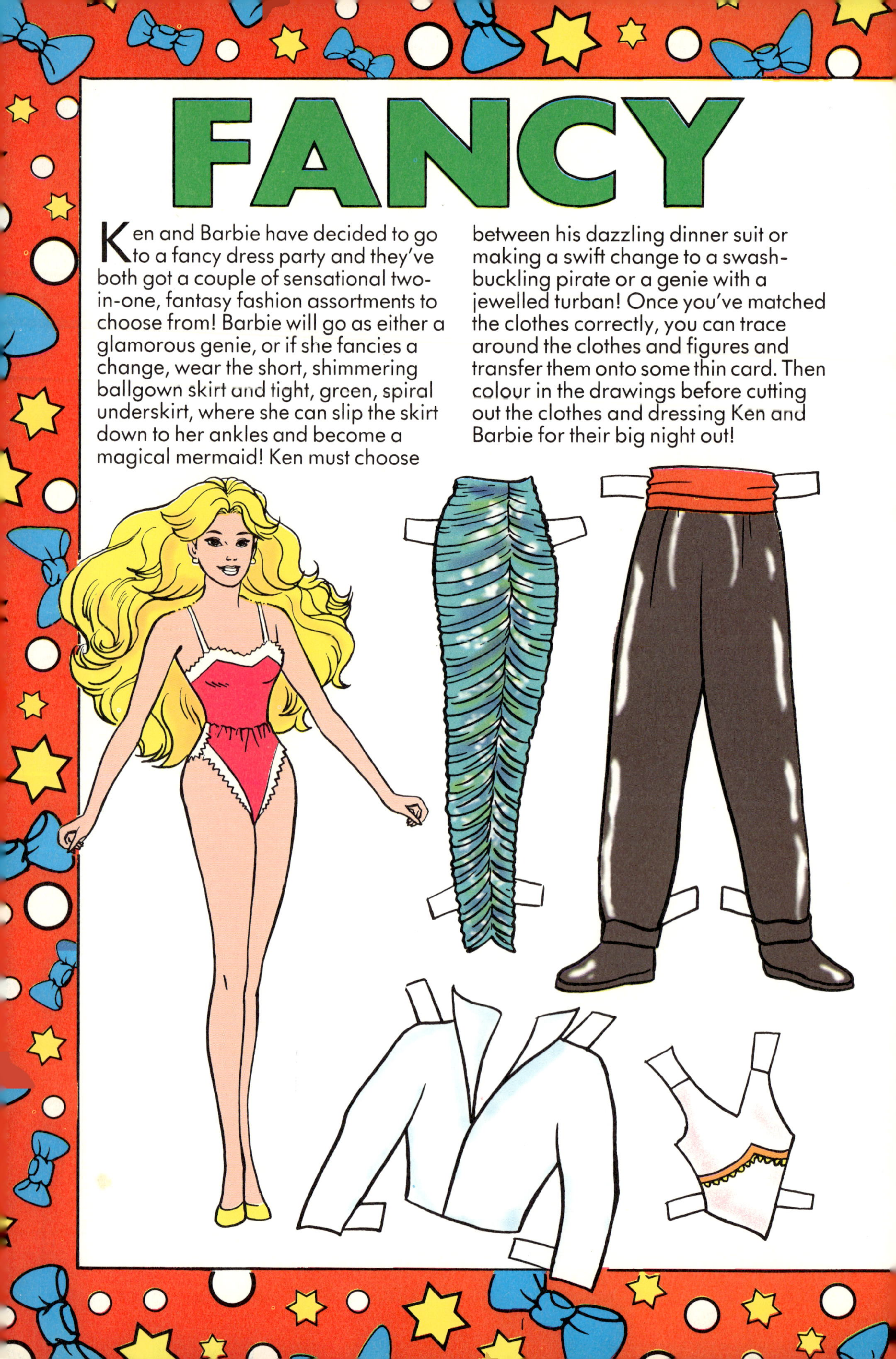

THAT!

Barbie™ IN HAIR-RAISING EXPERIENCE

CHRISTIE! MIDGE! THE MUSEUM SENT OVER OUR DRESSES! I CAN'T WAIT TO WEAR THEM!

WHEN WE VOLUNTEERED TO WORK AT THE ART OPENING TONIGHT, I DIDN'T KNOW THEY'D SEND US NEW OUTFITS!

LET'S TRY THEM ON!

AND I KNOW EXACTLY WHO TO CALL!
SOON...
THE MANE EVENT HAS ARRIVED!
UNIQUE MONIQUE WILL TURN OUR HAIR INTO WORKS OF ART!
UNIQUE MONIQUE
ARTIST·AT·WORK
CUTT'N UP
WHEN I'M THROUGH WITH YOUR TRESSES, NOBODY WILL NOTICE THOSE UGLY DRESSES!
I FORGOT TO MENTION UNIQUE MONIQUE LIKES TO RHYME!
THIS LICENSE MEANS I CAN DO ANYTHING I WANT WITH YOUR HAIR. MIDGE IS FIRST!
Artistic License
GULP
EEK! DON'T CUT IT TOO SHORT!
GASP!
DON'T RUIN MY HAIR!
CALM DOWN, MIDGE. MONIQUE HASN'T EVEN COMBED YOUR HAIR YET!
DON'T CURL IT TOO TIGHT!

HOW CAN I RELAX? MONIQUE COULD GIVE ME A CROSS BETWEEN A POODLE CUT, A RAT'S NEST, AND A BEEHIVE!
THAT WOULD BE TOO OLD-FASHIONED TO CUT WITH PASSION!
MAYBE MIDGE WOULD FEEL BETTER IF YOU DID ALL OF US AT THE SAME TIME!
YES!
I'LL TRY!
THREE AT ONCE. YOU'RE A WHIZ, MONIQUE!
WITH MY MAGIC GEL I'M A SCULPTOR OF HAIR EXTRAORDINAIRE!
I THINK SHE'S SCULPTING CONEHEADS.
MONIQUE'S MAGIC GEL
A DASH OF SPRAY, A SPRINKLE OF SPRITZ, THEN COMB GENTLY.
I LOVE EXPERIMENTS!
I HATE EXPERIMENTS!
SOON YOU'LL BE READY--
--JUST KEEP YOUR HEADS STEADY!

IT'S THE MOMENT OF TRUTH!

HEY, OUR HAIR LOOKS THE SAME AS IT DID BEFORE!
IT'S NOT FINISHED YET.

IT'LL BE DONE WHEN YOU GET TO THE ART OPENING.
WE'D BETTER HURRY. WE'RE LATE!

THANKS, MONIQUE! HOP IN, EVERYBODY!
I DON'T UNDERSTAND.

HOW WILL OUR HAIR FINISH ITSELF?
YOUR WORRIES ARE OVER, MIDGE...
VROOM!

...WE MADE IT!
MAYBE WE MADE IT... BUT OUR HAIR DIDN'T!
MUSEU
of ART

THE WIND BLEW OUR HAIR INTO THESE WILD SHAPES...
THESE HAIR-DO'S ARE HAIR-DON'T'S!
AND THEN MONIQUE'S STYLING GEL DRIED!
entrance

I THINK WE ALL LOOK GREAT!
LET'S GO IN AND SHOW OFF OUR HAIR, MIDGE!
O-OKAY.

I CAN'T HEAR WHAT THEY'RE SAYING, BUT I KNOW THEY HATE MY HAIR!
GORGEOUS!
SO ORIGINAL!
I LOVE THEIR HAIR!

I'M SO EMBARRASSED! I HATE MY HAIR!
MISS, EVERYONE IS TALKING ABOUT YOUR HAIR!
I KNOW.

IT LOOKS SENSATIONAL!
IT DOES?
IT GOES WITH MY EXHIBIT-- OUTER SPACES!

HEY, LOOK WHO'S HERE!
MONIQUE!
HI, GANG!

I DIDN'T KNOW YOU WERE COMING TO THE ART OPENING!
THE ARTIST IS A FRIEND OF MINE!
THAT'S WHY I GAVE YOU ALL HAIR-STYLES...
...TO GO WITH THIS EXHIBIT!
WE VOLUNTEERED TO WORK TONIGHT! LET'S FIND OUT WHAT THEY WANT US TO DO!
I CAN HELP YOU WITH THAT.
JUST FOLLOW ME!
EXHIBIT
MONIQUE IS FULL OF SURPRISES!
SOON...
BUT THIS IS THE BIGGEST SURPRISE OF ALL!
I DON'T BELIEVE IT WORKED OUT SO WELL!
THIS EXHIBIT IS OUT OF THIS WORLD...
AND SO IS OUR HAIR!
SENSATIONAL!
WORKS OF ART!
END.

RAZZLE

MAKING A NECKLACE AND BRACELET . . .

WHAT YOU NEED. . .

* A length of strong cotton, thin string or thin elastic.
* A selection of coloured buttons, beads and macaroni shapes.
* Glue.
* Different coloured paints and glitter.

WHAT YOU DO. . .

1. Collect together a selection of different shaped buttons, beads and macaroni pieces. They should all have holes in them through which you can thread your string.

2. If your selection is already colourful, leave them as they are. If not, using paint and a small brush, or a little bit of glue and some glitter, decorate your buttons, beads and macaroni.

3. Place the pieces you have chosen for your necklace and bracelet so that the colours and shapes alternate in an attractive way.

4. Measure a length of string around your wrist and allow another four inches. Do the same around your neck. Thread the buttons, beads and macaroni onto the two pieces of string in the order you have chosen. Tie the ends together and you have a bright and colourful necklace and bracelet to show to your friends!

MAKING A BROOCH. . .

WHAT YOU NEED. . .

- ★ A piece of strong card – the size of a birthday card.
- ★ Glue, scissors, a safety pin and sticky tape.
- ★ Silver foil, different coloured paints and glitter.

WHAT YOU DO. . .

1. Choose the shape you want for your brooch; either a square, circle or triangle. Cut the shape out of the card.

2. Cover the card with a bright colour, either using your paints or some silver foil wrapped over the edges and glued to the back.

Using a strong piece of sticky tape, stick the safety pin to the back of the card as shown in the diagram.

4. Decorate the front of the brooch, either by making patterns with different coloured paints or making a pattern with a thin line of glue and sprinkling on some glitter.

Wow! When you show off your brand new, sparkling jewellery to your friends, they'll think you're a real star!

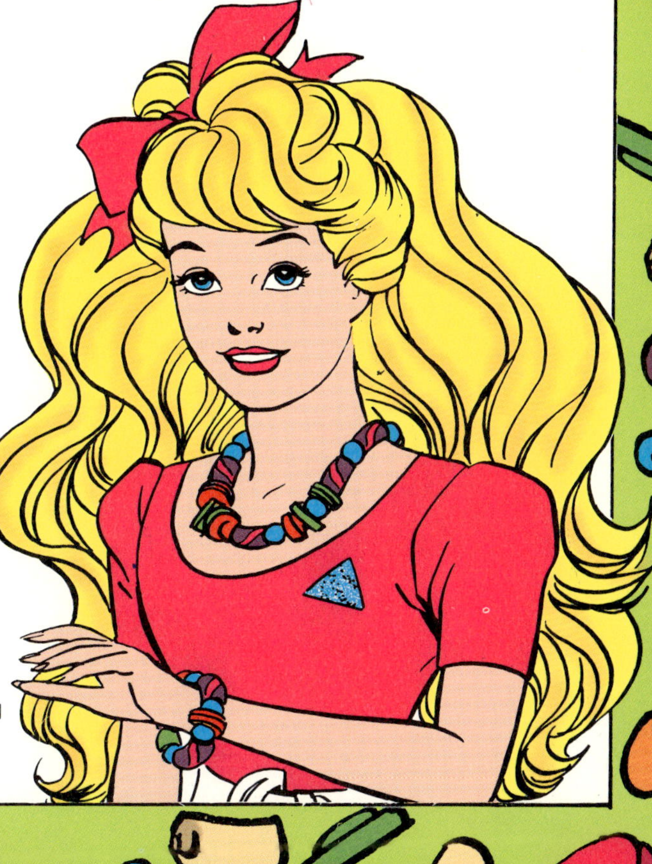